MW00914921

If Lost, Please Return to:

_____

Phone Number:

_____

Email:

_____

Credits:

Authored By:
David L. Convissar, MD

Assistant Author:
Victoria N. Nguyen, MD

Illustrations By:
Chaden Noureddine, BA
Michael Ye
Kathryn Ticehurst, MD

Editors:
Raymond Malapero, MD, MPH
Jean-Daniel Eloy, MD
Evelyne Gone, MD

First Edition:
March, 2020

Forward:

"I put together this guidebook because it's something I wish I had when I started my Anesthesia training. Something to ensure I got the most out of every experience inside and outside of the OR.

As anesthesia providers, we have a unique relationship with our patients in which we are their sole medical provider in their most vulnerable moments.

Because of this unique position, it is pivotal that we understand inside and out every drug, monitor, procedure, as well as any other tool that may be part of our repertoire in their management. I hope for this book to be the vessel to help guide you through your learning.

Remember that the patient on the table is someone's mom or dad, brother or sister, son or daughter. Remember that while you are a life-long learner, you should strive to be the kind of practitioner you would want taking care of you or your loved ones."

- *David L. Convissar, M.D.*

Table of Contents:

Pharmacology

Fluids

Monitors

Ventilator

Cardiac Anesthesia

Acute and Chronic Pain

Pediatrics

Obstetrics and Gynecology

Intraoperative Emergencies

Recovery Room

Cases

9

Propofol:

Mechanism of Action:

Dose(s):

Metabolism/Cessation of Action:

Onset/Duration of Action:

Cardiovascular Effects:

Respiratory Effects:

Nervous System Effects:

Other:

Etomidate:

Mechanism of Action:

Dose(s):

Metabolism/Cessation of Action:

Onset/Duration of Action:

Cardiovascular Effects:

Respiratory Effects:

Nervous System Effects:

Other:

11

Ketamine:

Mechanism of Action:

Dose(s):

Metabolism/Cessation of Action:

Onset/Duration of Action:

Cardiovascular Effects:

Respiratory Effects:

Nervous System Effects:

Other:

Dexmedetomidine:

Mechanism of Action:

Dose(s):

Metabolism/Cessation of Action:

Onset/Duration of Action:

Cardiovascular Effects:

Respiratory Effects:

Nervous System Effects:

Other:

Midazolam:

Mechanism of Action:

Dose(s):

Metabolism/Cessation of Action:

Onset/Duration of Action:

Cardiovascular Effects:

Respiratory Effects:

Nervous System Effects:

Other:

Induction Agent:

Mechanism of Action:

Dose(s):

Metabolism/Cessation of Action:

Onset/Duration of Action:

Cardiovascular Effects:

Respiratory Effects:

Nervous System Effects:

Other:

15

Induction Agent:

Mechanism of Action:

Dose(s):

Metabolism/Cessation of Action:

Onset/Duration of Action:

Cardiovascular Effects:

Respiratory Effects:

Nervous System Effects:

Other:

Nitrous Oxide:

MAC:

Vapor Pressure:

Blood:Gas Coefficient:

Mechanism of Action:

Cardiovascular Effects:

Respiratory Effects:

Central Nervous System Effects:

Other:

Isoflurane:

MAC:

Vapor Pressure:

Blood:Gas Coefficient:

Mechanism of Action:

Cardiovascular Effects:

Respiratory Effects:

Central Nervous System Effects:

Other:

Sevoflurane:

MAC:

Vapor Pressure:

Blood:Gas Coefficient:

Mechanism of Action:

Cardiovascular Effects:

Respiratory Effects:

Central Nervous System Effects:

Other:

Desflurane:

MAC:

Vapor Pressure:

Blood:Gas Coefficient:

Mechanism of Action:

Cardiovascular Effects:

Respiratory Effects:

Central Nervous System Effects:

Other:

Halothane:

MAC:

Vapor Pressure:

Blood:Gas Coefficient:

Mechanism of Action:

Cardiovascular Effects:

Respiratory Effects:

Central Nervous System Effects:

Other:

Volatile:

MAC:

Vapor Pressure:

Blood:Gas Coefficient:

Mechanism of Action:

Cardiovascular Effects:

Respiratory Effects:

Central Nervous System Effects:

Other:

Volatile:

MAC:

Vapor Pressure:

Blood:Gas Coefficient:

Mechanism of Action:

Cardiovascular Effects:

Respiratory Effects:

Central Nervous System Effects:

Other:

Rocuronium:

Mechanism of Action:

Metabolism/Cessation of Action:

Dose(s):

Onset/Duration of Action/Half Life:

High Yield Systemic Effects and Side Effects

Other:

Vecuronium:

Mechanism of Action:

Metabolism/Cessation of Action:

Dose(s):

Onset/Duration of Action/Half Life:

High Yield Systemic Effects and Side Effects

Other:

Atricurium:

Mechanism of Action:

Metabolism/Cessation of Action:

Dose(s):

Onset/Duration of Action/Half Life:

High Yield Systemic Effects and Side Effects

Other:

Cisatricurium:

Mechanism of Action:

Metabolism/Cessation of Action:

Dose(s):

Onset/Duration of Action/Half Life:

High Yield Systemic Effects and Side Effects

Other:

Pancuronium:

Mechanism of Action:

Metabolism/Cessation of Action:

Dose(s):

Onset/Duration of Action/Half Life:

High Yield Systemic Effects and Side Effects

Other:

Succinylcholine:

Mechanism of Action:

Metabolism/Cessation of Action:

Dose(s):

Onset/Duration of Action/Half Life:

High Yield Systemic Effects and Side Effects

Other:

Muscle Relaxant:

Mechanism of Action:

Metabolism/Cessation of Action:

Dose(s):

Onset/Duration of Action/Half Life:

High Yield Systemic Effects and Side Effects

Other:

Fentanyl:

Dose(s):

Onset/Duration of Action/Half Life:

Cardiovascular Effects:

Respiratory Effects:

Nervous System Effects:

High Yield Information/Other:

Hydromorphone:

Dose(s):

Onset/Duration of Action/Half Life:

Cardiovascular Effects:

Respiratory Effects:

Nervous System Effects:

High Yield Information/Other:

Morphine:

Dose(s):

Onset/Duration of Action/Half Life:

Cardiovascular Effects:

Respiratory Effects:

Nervous System Effects:

High Yield Information/Other:

Remifentanil:

Dose(s):

Onset/Duration of Action/Half Life:

Cardiovascular Effects:

Respiratory Effects:

Nervous System Effects:

High Yield Information/Other:

Oxycodone:

Dose(s):

Onset/Duration of Action/Half Life:

Cardiovascular Effects:

Respiratory Effects:

Nervous System Effects:

High Yield Information/Other:

Methadone:

Dose(s):

Onset/Duration of Action/Half Life:

Cardiovascular Effects:

Respiratory Effects:

Nervous System Effects:

High Yield Information/Other:

Narcotic:

Dose(s):

Onset/Duration of Action/Half Life:

Cardiovascular Effects:

Respiratory Effects:

Nervous System Effects:

High Yield Information/Other:

Narcotic:

Dose(s):

Onset/Duration of Action/Half Life:

Cardiovascular Effects:

Respiratory Effects:

Nervous System Effects:

High Yield Information/Other:

Narcotic:

Dose(s):

Onset/Duration of Action/Half Life:

Cardiovascular Effects:

Respiratory Effects:

Nervous System Effects:

High Yield Information/Other:

Acetaminophen:

Mechanism of Action:

Metabolism/Cessation of Action:

Dose(s):

Onset/Duration of Action/Half Life:

High Yield Information/Notes:

40

Toradol:

Mechanism of Action:

Metabolism/Cessation of Action:

Dose(s):

Onset/Duration of Action/Half Life:

High Yield Information/Notes:

Baclofen:

Mechanism of Action:

Metabolism/Cessation of Action:

Dose(s):

Onset/Duration of Action/Half Life:

High Yield Information/Notes:

Gabapentin:

Mechanism of Action:

Metabolism/Cessation of Action:

Dose(s):

Onset/Duration of Action/Half Life:

High Yield Information/Notes:

Ibuprofen:

Mechanism of Action:

Metabolism/Cessation of Action:

Dose(s):

Onset/Duration of Action/Half Life:

High Yield Information/Notes:

Non-Opioid Analgesic:

Mechanism of Action:

Metabolism/Cessation of Action:

Dose(s):

Onset/Duration of Action/Half Life:

High Yield Information/Notes:

Non-Opioid Analgesic:

Mechanism of Action:

Metabolism/Cessation of Action:

Dose(s):

Onset/Duration of Action/Half Life:

High Yield Information/Notes:

Non-Opioid Analgesic:

Mechanism of Action:

Metabolism/Cessation of Action:

Dose(s):

Onset/Duration of Action/Half Life:

High Yield Information/Notes:

Atropine:

Mechanism of Action:

Metabolism/Cessation of Action:

Dose(s):

Onset/Duration of Action/Half Life:

Cardiovascular Effects:

Respiratory Effects:

Nervous System Effects:

High Yield Information/Other:

Glycopyrrolate:

Mechanism of Action:

Metabolism/Cessation of Action:

Dose(s):

Onset/Duration of Action/Half Life:

Cardiovascular Effects:

Respiratory Effects:

Nervous System Effects:

High Yield Information/Other:

Scopolamine:

Mechanism of Action:

Metabolism/Cessation of Action:

Dose(s):

Onset/Duration of Action/Half Life:

Cardiovascular Effects:

Respiratory Effects:

Nervous System Effects:

High Yield Information/Other:

Anticholinergic:

Mechanism of Action:

Metabolism/Cessation of Action:

Dose(s):

Onset/Duration of Action/Half Life:

Cardiovascular Effects:

Respiratory Effects:

Nervous System Effects:

High Yield Information/Other:

Anticholinergic:

Mechanism of Action:

Metabolism/Cessation of Action:

Dose(s):

Onset/Duration of Action/Half Life:

Cardiovascular Effects:

Respiratory Effects:

Nervous System Effects:

High Yield Information/Other:

Neostigmine

Mechanism of Action:

Metabolism/Cessation of Action:

Dose(s):

Onset/Duration of Action/Half Life:

Cardiovascular Effects:

Respiratory Effects:

Nervous System Effects:

High Yield Information/Other:

Pyridostigmine

Mechanism of Action:

Metabolism/Cessation of Action:

Dose(s):

Onset/Duration of Action/Half Life:

Cardiovascular Effects:

Respiratory Effects:

Nervous System Effects:

High Yield Information/Other:

Physostigmine

Mechanism of Action:

Metabolism/Cessation of Action:

Dose(s):

Onset/Duration of Action/Half Life:

Cardiovascular Effects:

Respiratory Effects:

Nervous System Effects:

High Yield Information/Other:

Acetylcholinesterase Inhibitor:

Mechanism of Action:

Metabolism/Cessation of Action:

Dose(s):

Onset/Duration of Action/Half Life:

Cardiovascular Effects:

Respiratory Effects:

Nervous System Effects:

High Yield Information/Other:

Sugammadex:

Mechanism of Action:

Metabolism/Cessation of Action:

Dose(s):

Onset/Duration of Action/Half Life:

Cardiovascular Effects:

Respiratory Effects:

Nervous System Effects:

High Yield Information/Other:

Chloroprocaine:

Mechanism of Action:

Metabolism/Cessation of Action:

Dose(s):

Onset/Duration of Action/Half Life:

Cardiovascular Effects:

Respiratory Effects:

Nervous System Effects:

High Yield Information/Other:

Lidocaine:

Mechanism of Action:

Metabolism/Cessation of Action:

Dose(s):

Onset/Duration of Action/Half Life:

Cardiovascular Effects:

Respiratory Effects:

Nervous System Effects:

High Yield Information/Other:

Bupivacaine:

Mechanism of Action:

Metabolism/Cessation of Action:

Dose(s):

Onset/Duration of Action/Half Life:

Cardiovascular Effects:

Respiratory Effects:

Nervous System Effects:

High Yield Information/Other:

Ropivacaine:

Mechanism of Action:

Metabolism/Cessation of Action:

Dose(s):

Onset/Duration of Action/Half Life:

Cardiovascular Effects:

Respiratory Effects:

Nervous System Effects:

High Yield Information/Other:

Local Anesthetic:

Mechanism of Action:

Metabolism/Cessation of Action:

Dose(s):

Onset/Duration of Action/Half Life:

Cardiovascular Effects:

Respiratory Effects:

Nervous System Effects:

High Yield Information/Other:

Norepinephrine:

Mechanism of Action:

Dose(s):

Onset/Duration of Action/Half Life:

Cardiovascular Effects:

High Yield Information/Other:

Epinephrine:

Mechanism of Action:

Dose(s):

Onset/Duration of Action/Half Life:

Cardiovascular Effects:

High Yield Information/Other:

Dopamine:

Mechanism of Action:

Dose(s):

Onset/Duration of Action/Half Life:

Cardiovascular Effects:

High Yield Information/Other:

Dobutamine:

Mechanism of Action:

Dose(s):

Onset/Duration of Action/Half Life:

Cardiovascular Effects:

High Yield Information/Other:

Milrinone:

Mechanism of Action:

Dose(s):

Onset/Duration of Action/Half Life:

Cardiovascular Effects:

High Yield Information/Other:

Isoproterenol:

Mechanism of Action:

Dose(s):

Onset/Duration of Action/Half Life:

Cardiovascular Effects:

High Yield Information/Other:

Ephedrine:

Mechanism of Action:

Dose(s):

Onset/Duration of Action/Half Life:

Cardiovascular Effects:

High Yield Information/Other:

Phenylephrine:

Mechanism of Action:

Dose(s):

Onset/Duration of Action/Half Life:

Cardiovascular Effects:

High Yield Information/Other:

Vasopressin:

Mechanism of Action:

Dose(s):

Onset/Duration of Action/Half Life:

Cardiovascular Effects:

High Yield Information/Other:

Inotropic Agents/ Pressor:

Mechanism of Action:

Dose(s):

Onset/Duration of Action/Half Life:

Cardiovascular Effects:

High Yield Information/Other:

Albuterol:

Mechanism of Action:

Dose(s):

Onset/Duration of Action/Half Life:

High Yield Information/Other:

Ipratropium:

Mechanism of Action:

Dose(s):

Onset/Duration of Action/Half Life:

High Yield Information/Other:

Terbutaline:

Mechanism of Action:

Dose(s):

Onset/Duration of Action/Half Life:

High Yield Information/Other:

Bronchodilator:

Mechanism of Action:

Dose(s):

Onset/Duration of Action/Half Life:

High Yield Information/Other:

Metoprolol:

Mechanism of Action:

Dose(s):

Metabolism/Cessation of Action:

Onset/Duration of Action/Half Life:

High Yield Information/Other:

Labetalol:

Mechanism of Action:

Dose(s):

Metabolism/Cessation of Action:

Onset/Duration of Action/Half Life:

High Yield Information/Other:

Esmolol:

Mechanism of Action:

Dose(s):

Metabolism/Cessation of Action:

Onset/Duration of Action/Half Life:

High Yield Information/Other:

Hydralazine:

Mechanism of Action:

Dose(s):

Metabolism/Cessation of Action:

Onset/Duration of Action/Half Life:

High Yield Information/Other:

Nicardipine:

Mechanism of Action:

Dose(s):

Metabolism/Cessation of Action:

Onset/Duration of Action/Half Life:

High Yield Information/Other:

Nitroglycerine:

Mechanism of Action:

Dose(s):

Metabolism/Cessation of Action:

Onset/Duration of Action/Half Life:

High Yield Information/Other:

Nitroprusside:

Mechanism of Action:

Dose(s):

Metabolism/Cessation of Action:

Onset/Duration of Action/Half Life:

High Yield Information/Other:

Diltiazem:

Mechanism of Action:

Dose(s):

Metabolism/Cessation of Action:

Onset/Duration of Action/Half Life:

High Yield Information/Other:

Amiodarone:

Mechanism of Action:

Dose(s):

Metabolism/Cessation of Action:

Onset/Duration of Action/Half Life:

High Yield Information/Other:

Digoxin:

Mechanism of Action:

Dose(s):

Metabolism/Cessation of Action:

Onset/Duration of Action/Half Life:

High Yield Information/Other:

Ondansetron:

Mechanism of Action:

Dose(s):

Metabolism/Cessation of Action:

Onset/Duration of Action/Half Life:

High Yield Information/Other:

Dexamethasone:

Mechanism of Action:

Dose(s):

Metabolism/Cessation of Action:

Onset/Duration of Action/Half Life:

High Yield Information/Other:

Metoclopramide:

Mechanism of Action:

Dose(s):

Metabolism/Cessation of Action:

Onset/Duration of Action/Half Life:

High Yield Information/Other:

Prochlorperazine:

Mechanism of Action:

Dose(s):

Metabolism/Cessation of Action:

Onset/Duration of Action/Half Life:

High Yield Information/Other:

Pantoprazole:

Mechanism of Action:

Dose(s):

Metabolism/Cessation of Action:

Onset/Duration of Action/Half Life:

High Yield Information/Other:

Famotidine:

Mechanism of Action:

Dose(s):

Metabolism/Cessation of Action:

Onset/Duration of Action/Half Life:

High Yield Information/Other:

Oxytocin:

Mechanism of Action:

Dose(s):

Metabolism/Cessation of Action:

Onset/Duration of Action/Half Life:

High Yield Information/Other:

Methylergonovine:

Mechanism of Action:

Dose(s):

Metabolism/Cessation of Action:

Onset/Duration of Action/Half Life:

High Yield Information/Other:

Misoprostol:

Mechanism of Action:

Dose(s):

Metabolism/Cessation of Action:

Onset/Duration of Action/Half Life:

High Yield Information/Other:

Tranexamic Acid:

Mechanism of Action:

Dose(s):

Metabolism/Cessation of Action:

Onset/Duration of Action/Half Life:

High Yield Information/Other:

Aminocaproic Acid:

Mechanism of Action:

Dose(s):

Metabolism/Cessation of Action:

Onset/Duration of Action/Half Life:

High Yield Information/Other:

Aspirin:

Mechanism of Action:

Dose(s):

Metabolism/Cessation of Action:

Onset/Duration of Action/Half Life:

High Yield Information/Other:

Clopidogrel:

Mechanism of Action:

Dose(s):

Metabolism/Cessation of Action:

Onset/Duration of Action/Half Life:

High Yield Information/Other:

Warfarin:

Mechanism of Action:

Dose(s):

Metabolism/Cessation of Action:

Onset/Duration of Action/Half Life:

High Yield Information/Other:

Dabigatran:

Mechanism of Action:

Dose(s):

Metabolism/Cessation of Action:

Onset/Duration of Action/Half Life:

High Yield Information/Other:

Rivaroxaban:

Mechanism of Action:

Dose(s):

Metabolism/Cessation of Action:

Onset/Duration of Action/Half Life:

High Yield Information/Other:

Apixaban:

Mechanism of Action:

Dose(s):

Metabolism/Cessation of Action:

Onset/Duration of Action/Half Life:

High Yield Information/Other:

Fluids: Crystalloids
Normal Saline:

Ph-   Notes:
Osmolarity-
Sodium-
Chloride-
Potassium-
Magnesium-
Calcium-
Buffer-

Lactated Ringers: Notes:

Ph-
Osmolarity-
Sodium-
Chloride-
Potassium-
Magnesium-
Calcium-
Buffer-

Plasmalyte: Notes:

Ph-
Osmolarity-
Sodium-
Chloride-
Potassium-
Magnesium-
Calcium-
Buffer-

Hypertonic Saline: Notes:

Ph-
Osmolarity-
Sodium-
Chloride-
Potassium-
Magnesium-
Calcium-
Buffer-

Fluids: Crystalloids

_____:

Ph-
Osmolarity-
Sodium-
Chloride-
Potassium-
Magnesium-
Calcium-
Buffer-

Notes:

_____:

Ph-
Osmolarity-
Sodium-
Chloride-
Potassium-
Magnesium-
Calcium-
Buffer-

Notes:

_____:

Ph-
Osmolarity-
Sodium-
Chloride-
Potassium-
Magnesium-
Calcium-
Buffer-

Notes:

_____:

Ph-
Osmolarity-
Sodium-
Chloride-
Potassium-
Magnesium-
Calcium-
Buffer-

Notes:

Colloids

Albumin:

Hydroxyethyl Starch:

Dextran:

Blood Products:

Packed Red Blood Cells:

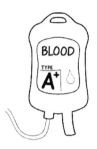

Fresh Frozen Plasma:

Platelets:

Cryoprecipitate:

107

Transfusion Reactions:

Febrile:

Allergic:

Acute Hemolytic:

Delayed Hemolytic:

Pulse Oximeter:

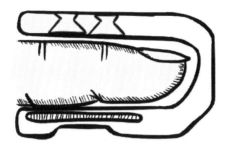

How it Works:

Pearls, Pitfalls, Troubleshooting and Notes:

Blood Pressure Cuff:

How it Works:

Pearls, Pitfalls, Troubleshooting and Notes:

Electrocardiogram:

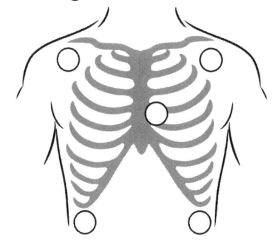

How it Works:

Pearls, Pitfalls, Troubleshooting and Notes:

111

Capnograph:

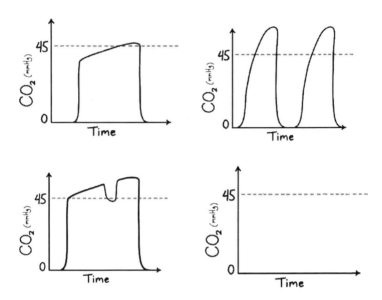

How it Works:

Pearls, Pitfalls, Troubleshooting and Notes:

Temperature Probe:

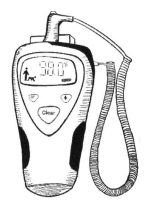

Core Temperatures and Non-core Temperatures

How it Works:

Pearls, Pitfalls, Troubleshooting and Notes:

Arterial Line:

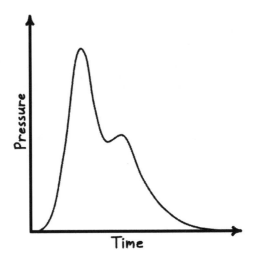

How it Works:

Troubleshooting:

Pearls, Pitfalls, Troubleshooting and Notes:

Central Venous Oxygen Monitor:

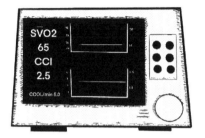

How it Works:

Causes for Decreases and Why:

Causes for Increases and Why:

Twitch Monitor and Train of Four:

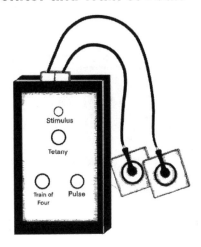

How it Works:

Causes for Decreases and Why:

Causes for Increases and Why:

116

Thromboelastogram:

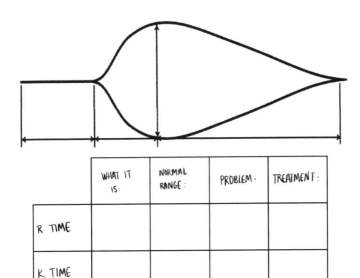

	WHAT IT IS:	NORMAL RANGE:	PROBLEM.	TREATMENT:
R TIME				
K TIME				
ALPHA (α) ANGLE				
MAXIMUM AMPLITUDE				
LYSIS AT 30 MINUTES				

Notes:

Basic Ventilator Settings:

Volume Control/Pressure Control:

Synchronized Intermittent Mandatory Ventilation:

Pressure Support:

TEE View:

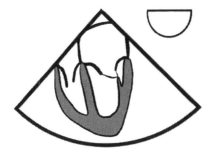

TEE View:

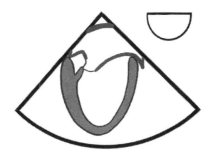

TEE View:

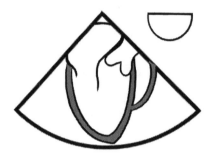

TEE View:

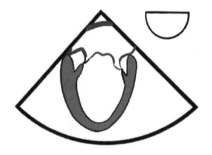

TEE View:

TEE View:

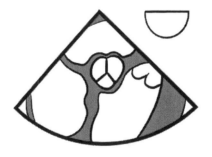

TEE View:

TEE View:

TEE View:

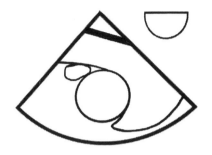

TEE View:

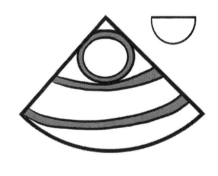

TEE View:

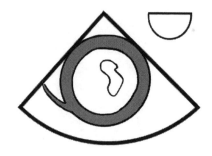

TEE View:

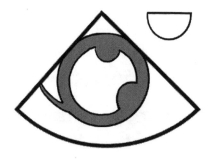

124

TEE View:

TEE View:

TEE View:

TEE View:

TEE View:

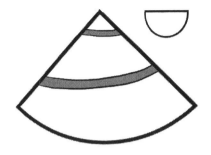

TEE View:

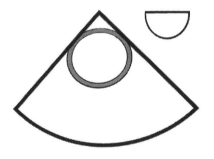

TEE View:

TEE View:

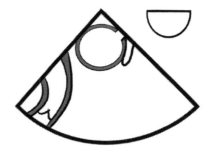

Normal Cardiac Values:

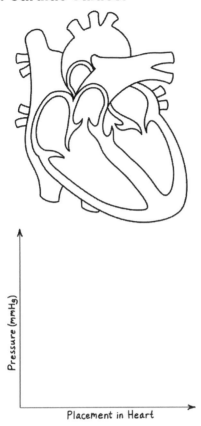

Notes:

Pacemaker:

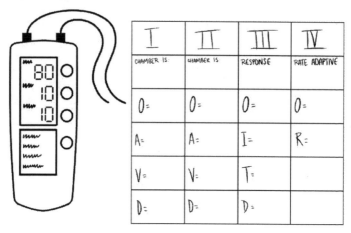

I	II	III	IV
CHAMBER IS:	CHAMBER IS:	RESPONSE	RATE ADAPTIVE
O =	O =	O =	O =
A =	A =	I =	R =
V =	V =	T =	
D =	D =	D =	

Notes:

130

Block: Interscalene

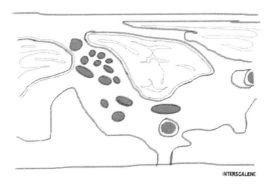

INTERSCALENE

Set Up/Medications/etc.:

Technique:

Indications/Contraindications:

Nerves Blocked/Notes:

Block: Supraclavicular

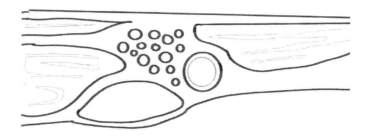

Supraclavicular

Set Up/Medications/etc.:

Technique:

Indications/Contraindications:

Nerves Blocked/Notes:

132

Block: Infraclavicular

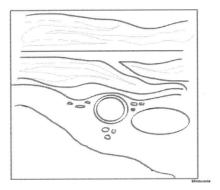

Set Up/Medications/etc.:

Technique:

Indications/Contraindications:

Nerves Blocked/Notes:

133

Block: Axillary

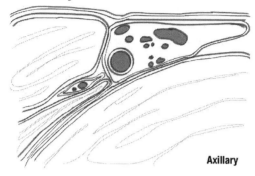

Axillary

Set Up/Medications/etc.:

Technique:

Indications/Contraindications:

Nerves Blocked/Notes:

Block: Femoral

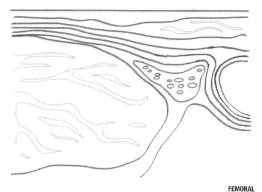

FEMORAL

Set Up/Medications/etc.:

Technique:

Indications/Contraindications:

Nerves Blocked/Notes:

135

Block: Popliteal/Sciatic

POPLITEAL (SCIATIC)

Set Up/Medications/etc.:

Technique:

Indications/Contraindications:

Nerves Blocked/Notes:

Block:

Set Up/Medications/etc.:

Technique:

Indications/Contraindications:

Nerves Blocked/Notes:

Block:

Set Up/Medications/etc.:

Technique:

Indications/Contraindications:

Nerves Blocked/Notes:

Opioid Equianalgesic Table:

Drug	IV Dose	Oral Dose
Morphine	10mg	30mg
Fentanyl		
Hydromorphone		
Oxycodone		
Meperidine		
Methadone		

Notes:

Patient Controlled Analgesia

Indications/Contraindications:

Drug Choice/Dose/Lockout:

Continuous/Non-Continuous Dosing:

Patient Controlled Epidural Analgesia

Indications/Contraindications:

Drug Choice/Dose/Lockout:

Continuous/Non-Continuous Dosing:

General Pain Notes

General Pain Notes

Pediatrics:

Differences in Neonatal Anatomy:

Induction Techniques:

Major Drug Dosing:

Pediatrics:

Fetal Circulation:

Pediatric Cardiac Norms:

Age	Heart Rate	Blood Pressure
Neonates		
1month – 1 year		
1 year – 3 years		

Notes:

Pediatrics:

Pediatric Endotracheal Tube Sizing:

Age	Tube Size (Cuffed)	Tube Size (Uncuffed)
Neonatal		
1 month- 6 months		
7 months to 1 year		

Notes:

General Pediatrics Notes

General Pediatrics Notes

Physiologic Changes of Pregnancy:

Cardiovascular:

Hematologic:

Airway:

Respiratory:

Other:

Lumbar Epidural:

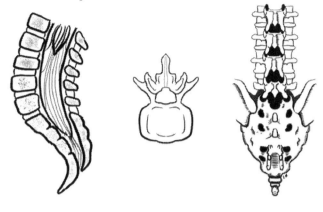

Set Up/Medications/etc.:

Technique and Doses:

Indications/Contraindications:

Notes:

Spinal:

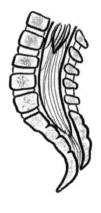  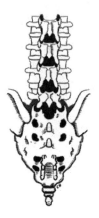

Set Up/Medications/etc.:

Technique and Doses:

Indications/Contraindications:

Notes:

Combined Spinal/Epidural:

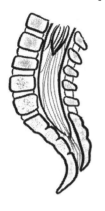  

Set Up/Medications/etc.:

Technique and Doses:

Indications/Contraindications:

Notes:

151

Epidural Alternatives:

General Obstetrical Anesthesia Notes

General Obstetrical Anesthesia Notes

Emergency: Pneumothorax

Pathophysiology:

Signs and Symptoms:

Differential:

Management:

Note:

Emergency: Malignant Hyperthermia

Pathophysiology:

Signs and Symptoms:

Differential:

Management:

Note:

Emergency: Massive Hemorrhage/MTP

Pathophysiology:

Signs and Symptoms:

Differential:

Management:

Note:

Emergency: Bronchospasm

Pathophysiology:

Signs and Symptoms:

Differential:

Management:

Note:

Emergency: Methemoglobinemia

Pathophysiology:

Signs and Symptoms:

Differential:

Management:

Note:

Emergency: Carbon Monoxide Poisoning

Pathophysiology:

Signs and Symptoms:

Differential:

Management:

Note:

Emergency: Local Anesthetic Systemic Toxicity Syndrome

Pathophysiology:

Signs and Symptoms:

Differential:

Management:

Note:

Emergency: Venous Air Embolism

Pathophysiology:

Signs and Symptoms:

Differential:

Management:

Note:

Emergency: Laryngospasm

Pathophysiology:

Signs and Symptoms:

Differential:

Management:

Note:

Emergency: Shockable Cardiac Arrest

Pathophysiology:

Signs and Symptoms:

Differential:

Management:

Note:

Emergency: Non-Shockable Cardiac Arrest

Pathophysiology:

Signs and Symptoms:

Differential:

Management:

Note:

165

Emergency: Pulmonary Embolism

Pathophysiology:

Signs and Symptoms:

Differential:

Management:

Note:

Emergency: Amniotic Fluid Embolism

Pathophysiology:

Signs and Symptoms:

Differential:

Management:

Note:

Emergency: Placenta Abruptio

Pathophysiology:

Signs and Symptoms:

Differential:

Management:

Note:

Emergency: Uterine Rupture

Pathophysiology:

Signs and Symptoms:

Differential:

Management:

Note:

Emergency:

Pathophysiology:

Signs and Symptoms:

Differential:

Management:

Note:

Emergency:

Pathophysiology:

Signs and Symptoms:

Differential:

Management:

Note:

Emergency:

Pathophysiology:

Signs and Symptoms:

Differential:

Management:

Note:

Difficult Airway Algorithm:

Recovery Room:

Hypoxemia

Hemodynamic Instability

Altered Mental Status/ Delirium

Post-Operative Nausea/ Vomiting

Discharge Criteria

174

General Recovery Room Notes:

Case Type:

Setup:

Induction Technique:

Preoperative Considerations:

Intraoperative Considerations:

Postoperative Considerations:

Notes/Diagrams/Other:

Case Type:

Setup:

Induction Technique:

Preoperative Considerations:

Intraoperative Considerations:

Postoperative Considerations:

Notes/Diagrams/Other:

Case Type:

Setup:

Induction Technique:

Preoperative Considerations:

Intraoperative Considerations:

Postoperative Considerations:

Notes/Diagrams/Other:

Case Type:

Setup:

Induction Technique:

Preoperative Considerations:

Intraoperative Considerations:

Postoperative Considerations:

Notes/Diagrams/Other:

Case Type:

Setup:

Induction Technique:

Preoperative Considerations:

Intraoperative Considerations:

Postoperative Considerations:

Notes/Diagrams/Other:

Case Type:

Setup:

Induction Technique:

Preoperative Considerations:

Intraoperative Considerations:

Postoperative Considerations:

Notes/Diagrams/Other:

Case Type:

Setup:

Induction Technique:

Preoperative Considerations:

Intraoperative Considerations:

Postoperative Considerations:

Notes/Diagrams/Other:

Case Type:

Setup:

Induction Technique:

Preoperative Considerations:

Intraoperative Considerations:

Postoperative Considerations:

Notes/Diagrams/Other:

Case Type:

Setup:

Induction Technique:

Preoperative Considerations:

Intraoperative Considerations:

Postoperative Considerations:

Notes/Diagrams/Other:

Case Type:

Setup:

Induction Technique:

Preoperative Considerations:

Intraoperative Considerations:

Postoperative Considerations:

Notes/Diagrams/Other:

Case Type:

Setup:

Induction Technique:

Preoperative Considerations:

Intraoperative Considerations:

Postoperative Considerations:

Notes/Diagrams/Other:

Case Type:

Setup:

Induction Technique:

Preoperative Considerations:

Intraoperative Considerations:

Postoperative Considerations:

Notes/Diagrams/Other:

Case Type:

Setup:

Induction Technique:

Preoperative Considerations:

Intraoperative Considerations:

Postoperative Considerations:

Notes/Diagrams/Other:

Case Type:

Setup:

Induction Technique:

Preoperative Considerations:

Intraoperative Considerations:

Postoperative Considerations:

Notes/Diagrams/Other:

Case Type:

Setup:

Induction Technique:

Preoperative Considerations:

Intraoperative Considerations:

Postoperative Considerations:

Notes/Diagrams/Other:

Case Type:

Setup:

Induction Technique:

Preoperative Considerations:

Intraoperative Considerations:

Postoperative Considerations:

Notes/Diagrams/Other:

Case Type:

Setup:

Induction Technique:

Preoperative Considerations:

Intraoperative Considerations:

Postoperative Considerations:

Notes/Diagrams/Other:

Case Type:

Setup:

Induction Technique:

Preoperative Considerations:

Intraoperative Considerations:

Postoperative Considerations:

Notes/Diagrams/Other:

Case Type:

Setup:

Induction Technique:

Preoperative Considerations:

Intraoperative Considerations:

Postoperative Considerations:

Notes/Diagrams/Other:

Case Type:

Setup:

Induction Technique:

Preoperative Considerations:

Intraoperative Considerations:

Postoperative Considerations:

Notes/Diagrams/Other:

Case Type:

Setup:

Induction Technique:

Preoperative Considerations:

Intraoperative Considerations:

Postoperative Considerations:

Notes/Diagrams/Other:

Case Type:

Setup:

Induction Technique:

Preoperative Considerations:

Intraoperative Considerations:

Postoperative Considerations:

Notes/Diagrams/Other:

Case Type:

Setup:

Induction Technique:

Preoperative Considerations:

Intraoperative Considerations:

Postoperative Considerations:

Notes/Diagrams/Other:

Case Type:

Setup:

Induction Technique:

Preoperative Considerations:

Intraoperative Considerations:

Postoperative Considerations:

Notes/Diagrams/Other:

Case Type:

Setup:

Induction Technique:

Preoperative Considerations:

Intraoperative Considerations:

Postoperative Considerations:

Notes/Diagrams/Other:

Case Type:

Setup:

Induction Technique:

Preoperative Considerations:

Intraoperative Considerations:

Postoperative Considerations:

Notes/Diagrams/Other:

Case Type:

Setup:

Induction Technique:

Preoperative Considerations:

Intraoperative Considerations:

Postoperative Considerations:

Notes/Diagrams/Other:

Case Type:

Setup:

Induction Technique:

Preoperative Considerations:

Intraoperative Considerations:

Postoperative Considerations:

Notes/Diagrams/Other:

Case Type:

Setup:

Induction Technique:

Preoperative Considerations:

Intraoperative Considerations:

Postoperative Considerations:

Notes/Diagrams/Other:

204

Case Type:

Setup:

Induction Technique:

Preoperative Considerations:

Intraoperative Considerations:

Postoperative Considerations:

Notes/Diagrams/Other:

Case Type:

Setup:

Induction Technique:

Preoperative Considerations:

Intraoperative Considerations:

Postoperative Considerations:

Notes/Diagrams/Other:

Case Type:

Setup:

Induction Technique:

Preoperative Considerations:

Intraoperative Considerations:

Postoperative Considerations:

Notes/Diagrams/Other:

Case Type:

Setup:

Induction Technique:

Preoperative Considerations:

Intraoperative Considerations:

Postoperative Considerations:

Notes/Diagrams/Other:

Case Type:

Setup:

Induction Technique:

Preoperative Considerations:

Intraoperative Considerations:

Postoperative Considerations:

Notes/Diagrams/Other:

Case Type:

Setup:

Induction Technique:

Preoperative Considerations:

Intraoperative Considerations:

Postoperative Considerations:

Notes/Diagrams/Other:

Case Type:

Setup:

Induction Technique:

Preoperative Considerations:

Intraoperative Considerations:

Postoperative Considerations:

Notes/Diagrams/Other:

Case Type:

Setup:

Induction Technique:

Preoperative Considerations:

Intraoperative Considerations:

Postoperative Considerations:

Notes/Diagrams/Other:

Case Type:

Setup:

Induction Technique:

Preoperative Considerations:

Intraoperative Considerations:

Postoperative Considerations:

Notes/Diagrams/Other:

Case Type:

Setup:

Induction Technique:

Preoperative Considerations:

Intraoperative Considerations:

Postoperative Considerations:

Notes/Diagrams/Other:

Case Type:

Setup:

Induction Technique:

Preoperative Considerations:

Intraoperative Considerations:

Postoperative Considerations:

Notes/Diagrams/Other:

Case Type:

Setup:

Induction Technique:

Preoperative Considerations:

Intraoperative Considerations:

Postoperative Considerations:

Notes/Diagrams/Other:

Case Type:

Setup:

Induction Technique:

Preoperative Considerations:

Intraoperative Considerations:

Postoperative Considerations:

Notes/Diagrams/Other:

Case Type:

Setup:

Induction Technique:

Preoperative Considerations:

Intraoperative Considerations:

Postoperative Considerations:

Notes/Diagrams/Other:

Case Type:

Setup:

Induction Technique:

Preoperative Considerations:

Intraoperative Considerations:

Postoperative Considerations:

Notes/Diagrams/Other:

Case Type:

Setup:

Induction Technique:

Preoperative Considerations:

Intraoperative Considerations:

Postoperative Considerations:

Notes/Diagrams/Other:

Case Type:

Setup:

Induction Technique:

Preoperative Considerations:

Intraoperative Considerations:

Postoperative Considerations:

Notes/Diagrams/Other:

Case Type:

Setup:

Induction Technique:

Preoperative Considerations:

Intraoperative Considerations:

Postoperative Considerations:

Notes/Diagrams/Other:

Case Type:

Setup:

Induction Technique:

Preoperative Considerations:

Intraoperative Considerations:

Postoperative Considerations:

Notes/Diagrams/Other:

Case Type:

Setup:

Induction Technique:

Preoperative Considerations:

Intraoperative Considerations:

Postoperative Considerations:

Notes/Diagrams/Other:

Case Type:

Setup:

Induction Technique:

Preoperative Considerations:

Intraoperative Considerations:

Postoperative Considerations:

Notes/Diagrams/Other:

Equations:

Alveolar Gas Equation:

$$\sqrt{\frac{x+\frac{1}{2}z^2}{a^2}} \cdot \frac{2}{x^2}^1 = \frac{\left(x^2+z^2+y^2-a^2\right)\left(y^2-z^2\right)}{\sqrt{3}y-2a^2\cdot\frac{x}{3}}$$

Arterial Oxygen Content:

Dead Space:

Shunt Fraction:

Airway Resistance / Poiseuille's Law:

Law of Laplace:

Reynold's Equation:

Static Compliance:

226

Dynamic Compliance:

Transpulmonary Pressure:

Predicted PaO2 by Age:

Boyle's Law:

Henry's Law:

Myocardial Perfusion Pressure:

Arterial Oxygen Content:

Cardiac Index:

Stroke Volume:

Systemic Vascular Resistance:

Pulmonary Vascular Resistance:

Cerebral Perfusion Pressure:

Maximum Allowable Blood Loss:

Volume of Distribution:

Made in the USA
Middletown, DE
14 December 2024

66975716R00137